PENGUINS
CLOSEUP

Lorna Hendry

W9-ATM-429

wild dog

PENGUINS are birds. They cannot fly, but they are very good swimmers. There are 17 different kinds of penguins.

PENGUINS are only found in the Southern Hemisphere. Some penguins live in Antarctica, which is the coldest place on Earth.

PENGUINS often live in very large groups called colonies. Millions of birds can live in one colony.

PENGUINS have excellent eyesight. They can see clearly under water as well as on land.

PENGUINS can swim faster and dive deeper than any other bird. Their wings act as flippers and their waterproof feathers keep their skin dry. A thick layer of fat keeps them warm in the cold water.

PENGUINS are very well camouflaged when they are swimming. The dark feathers on their back make it hard to see them from above.

From below, their white feathers blend into the sunshine, hiding them from predators underneath.

PENGUINS find their chicks by listening for each baby's unique call.

PENGUINS feed their babies by coughing up food from their stomachs. They pour the mixture into the chick's beak.

PENGUINS have to protect their eggs and chicks from birds of prey, such as eagles and hawks.

PENGUINS are hunted by leopard seals, sharks, and killer whales.

EMPEROR PENGUINS are the biggest of all the penguins. They can hold their breath for 20 minutes when they are diving.

Emperor Penguin chicks sit on their parents' feet for 50 days after they hatch. The ice is too cold for the baby penguins to stand on.

FAIRY PENGUINS
(also called Little
Blue Penguins)
are the smallest of
all the penguins.
They are only
13 inches tall.

MAGELLANIC PENGUINS and Fairy Penguins dig holes called burrows. This is where they lay their eggs.

GALAPAGOS PENGUINS live close to the Equator. They lay their eggs in caves to protect them from the hot sun. They are the rarest of all penguins.

CHINSTRAP PENGUINS live on icebergs in winter. They get their name from the black band under their beaks.

ROCKHOPPER PENGUINS
live in steep, rocky
places. They hop
from rock to rock
to get around.

Rockhoppers are very loud and noisy. They are not scared of other animals and will attack anything that upsets them.

YELLOW EYED PENGUINS live in New Zealand. Like many penguins, they are an endangered species.

The biggest threat to the survival of penguins comes from human activities, such as an oil spill or plastic litter.

First published in 2013 by

 wild dog

54A Alexandra Parade
Clifton Hill Vic 3068
Australia
+61 3 9419 9406
dog@wdog.com.au
wdog.com.au

Copyright text © Eion Pty Ltd 2013
Copyright layout and design © Eion Pty Ltd 2013

All rights reserved. Apart from any fair dealing for the purpose of study, research, criticism or review, as permitted under the Copyright Act, no part of this book may be reproduced by any process, stored in a retrieval system, or transmitted in any form, without permission of the copyright owner. All enquiries should be made to the publisher at the address above.

Printed and bound in China by Everbest Printing International.

Distributed in the U.S.A. by
Scholastic Inc.
New York, NY 10012

ISBN: 9781742032832 (pbk.)

5 4 3 2 1   13 14 15 16 17 18

PHOTO CREDITS:
All images courtesy of Shutterstock.
Photographers: Front Cover Jan Martin Will; p 1 Ronsmith; p 2-3 steve estvanik; p 4-5 Rich Lindie; p 6 Janelle Lugge; p 7 Christian Musat p 8-9 Raywoo; p 10 Leksele; p 11 Josh Anon; p 12 Vladimir Sazonov; p 13 Jan Martin Will; p 14 Gentoo Multimedia Limited; p 15 Gentoo Multimedia Limited; p 16 Khoroshunova Olga; p 17 Yevgenia Gorbulsky; p 18 Alfie Photography; p 19 Mogens Trolle; p 20-21 Johnathan Esper; p 22 Bjorn Stefanson; p 23 fish1715; p 24 Eric Isselee; Back cover Mariusz Potocki

Wild Dog would like to thank
Dr. Mark Norman for his factual check
of this book.

MIX
Paper from
responsible sources
FSC® C021256
FSC
www.fsc.org

FSC® is a non-profit international organisation established to promote the responsible management of the world's forests.

GLOSSARY:

BIRD OF PREY: A bird that hunts and eats animals.

CAMOUFLAGE: Markings on an animal that help it blend into the background.

ENDANGERED SPECIES: A type of animal that is so rare that it might disappear.

EQUATOR: The line on a map that goes around the center of the Earth.

POLLUTION: Anything that makes the air, land, or sea dirty.

UNIQUE: One of a kind.

First published in 2013 by

 wild dog

54A Alexandra Parade
Clifton Hill Vic 3068
Australia
+61 3 9419 9406
dog@wdog.com.au
wdog.com.au

Copyright text © Eion Pty Ltd 2013
Copyright layout and design © Eion Pty Ltd 2013

All rights reserved. Apart from any fair dealing for the purpose of study, research, criticism or review, as permitted under the Copyright Act, no part of this book may be reproduced by any process, stored in a retrieval system, or transmitted in any form, without permission of the copyright owner. All enquiries should be made to the publisher at the address above.

Printed and bound in China by Everbest Printing International.

Distributed in the U.S.A. by
Scholastic Inc.
New York, NY 10012

ISBN: 9781742032832 (pbk.)

5 4 3 2 1   13 14 15 16 17 18

PHOTO CREDITS:
All images courtesy of Shutterstock.
Front cover Sergey Uryadnikov; p 1 Iakov Filimonov; p 2-3 La Nau de Fotografia; p 4 Wild Arctic Pictures; p 5 Yvonne Pijnenburg-Schonewille; p 6-7 Joshua Haviv; p 8-9 Sergey Uryadnikov; p 10-11 Stefan Redel; p 12 Zhiltsov Alexandr; p 13 Jody Dingle; p 14 Sergey Uryadnikov; p 15 Sergey Skleznev; p 16-17 Sergey Uryadnikov; p 18 Tatiana Belova; p 19 Andrew Astbury; p 20-21 Antoine Beyeler; p 22-23 Yvonne Pijnenburg-Schonewille; p 24 Susan Flashman; Back cover Kathyana

Wild Dog would like to thank
Dr. Mark Norman for his factual check
of this book.

MIX
Paper from
responsible sources
FSC® C021256
FSC
www.fsc.org

FSC® is a non-profit international organisation established to promote the responsible management of the world's forests.

GLOSSARY:

ARCTIC: the region around the North Pole.

PREDATOR: an animal that hunts another animal for food.

PREY: an animal that is hunted by another animal.

POLAR BEARS are vulnerable to the changing climate. As the planet warms and the ice melts, the bears will have less space to live, breed, and hunt.

POLAR BEARS usually move quite slowly on land. However, when chasing prey, polar bears are capable of bursts of speed. They can run up to 25 miles an hour over short distances.

POLAR BEARS and Arctic foxes live in many of the same environments. Sometimes, Arctic foxes travel behind polar bears and scavenge scraps of food that the bears leave behind.

POLAR BEARS have an excellent sense of smell. A polar bear can smell a seal from a mile away. They can also smell prey that is hiding under the snow!

POLAR BEAR babies are tiny when they are born – no bigger than a rat! But with lots of food they can grow very quickly, becoming the size of a full-grown human in a year.

Cubs will stay with their mom for up to two-and-a-half years.

POLAR BEAR females usually have two cubs. Cubs are born in caves that the female bears dig into the snow.

POLAR BEARS can swallow big chunks of food and don't usually need to chew very much.

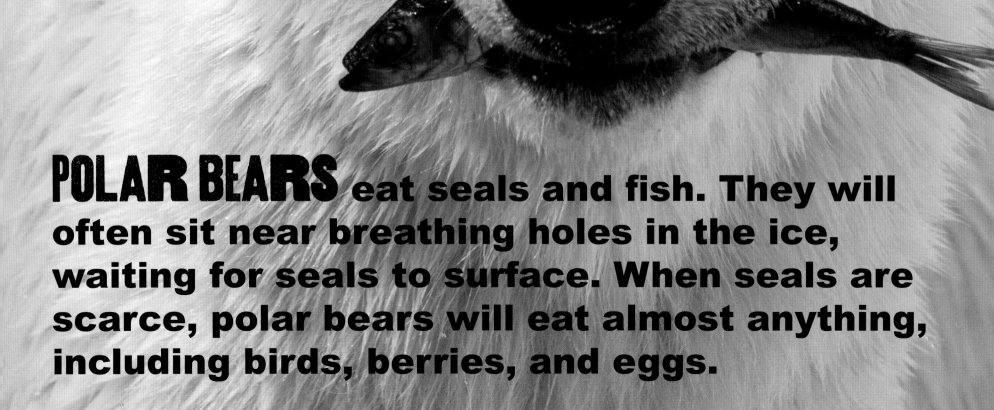

POLAR BEARS eat seals and fish. They will often sit near breathing holes in the ice, waiting for seals to surface. When seals are scarce, polar bears will eat almost anything, including birds, berries, and eggs.

POLAR BEARS have huge, wide paws with rough pads underneath. These paws act like snow shoes, and are perfect for walking across the snow and ice without sinking or slipping. Polar bear paws can measure up to 12 inches across.

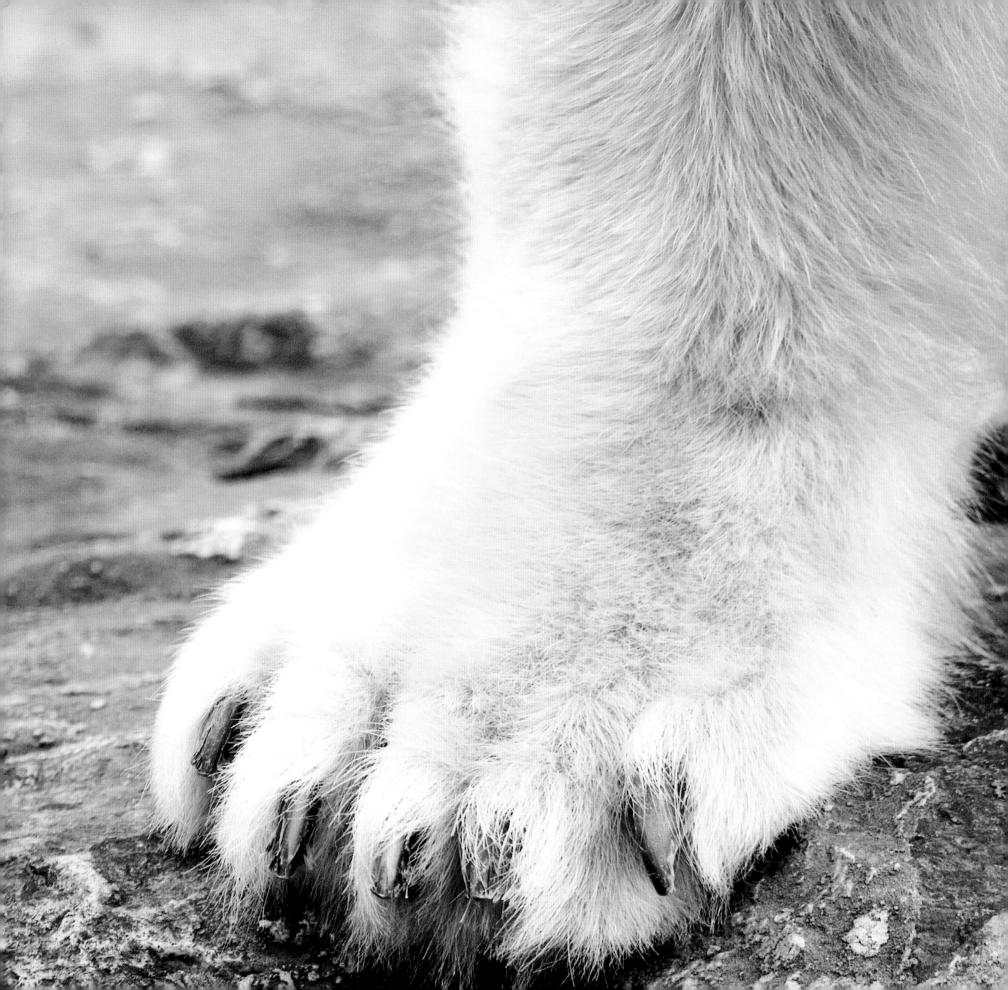

The only parts of the bear not covered with fur are the nose and footpads. Their skin is actually black.

POLAR BEAR fur is oily and water repellent, which is perfect for the cold, wet conditions where they live. Their fur is not actually white – each hair is a hollow tube which reflects the light, making the bears appear white. A thick, woolly undercoat helps keep them warm.

POLAR BEARS are great swimmers, and they can swim for long distances. They have been known to swim over 90 miles at a time. When swimming, their front paws act like paddles, propelling the bear through the water. Their hind paws are used to steer.

The scientific name for **POLAR BEARS** is *Ursus maritimus*. It means 'sea bear'.

POLAR BEARS are the largest land predators in the world. Males can grow 10 feet tall and weigh over 1,300 pounds. Females are usually smaller than male bears.

POLAR BEARS live in the cold northern parts of the world. They can be found in the Arctic, Alaska, Canada, Russia, Greenland, and Norway. Penguins live in southern parts of the world – in the wild, polar bears and penguins would never meet!

CLOSE
UP

POLAR
BEARS

Melissa Keil

CLOSEUP

wild dog